SUPER
BASEBALL
INFOGRAPHICS

Eric Braun

graphics by
Laura Westlund

Lerner Publications • Minneapolis

Lerner Publications Company
A division of Lerner Publishing Group, Inc.
241 First Avenue North
Minneapolis, MN USA 55401

For reading levels and more information, look up this title at
www.lernerbooks.com.

Main text set in Univers LT Std 12/15.
Typeface provided by Adobe Systems.

Library of Congress Cataloging-in-Publication Data

Braun, Eric, 1971–
    Super baseball infographics / by Eric Braun.
        pages   cm. — (Super sports infographics)
    Includes index.
    ISBN 978-1-4677-5232-9 (lib. bdg. : alk. paper)
    ISBN 978-1-4677-7574-8 (pbk.)
    ISBN 978-1-4677-6275-5 (EB pdf)
    1. Baseball—Graphic methods—Juvenile literature. I. Title.
GV867.B73 2015
796.357—dc23   2014009409

Manufactured in the United States of America
2 – PC – 4/1/16

CONTENTS

Introduction

LET'S PLAY BALL!

Are you a baseball fan? Take this quiz to test your love of the game.

1. Have you ever wondered why a curveball curves?

2. Do you dream of becoming the all-time home run champion?

3. Do you ever wonder what's inside of a baseball?

4. Can you name the most successful teams in Major League Baseball (MLB) history?

Did you answer yes to any of those questions?

IF SO, STEP UP TO THE PLATE!

You're ready to dig deeper into America's national pastime. There's a reason this sport has been so popular for more than a hundred years. It's complicated and challenging. It's filled with rich history, colorful characters, and funky physics. Most of all, it's a lot of fun—to watch and to play.

Some baseball fans study this game for many years. You don't have to do that (unless you want to). But learning more about baseball can help you enjoy it more as a player and a fan. Charts, graphs, and other infographics are a great place to start. Are you ready to take a swing? Turn the page!

INSIDE BASEBALL

Let's take an insider's look at baseball. No, you don't get to go inside an MLB locker room. We're talking about the inside of an *actual* baseball.

Baseballs are made of a lot of different parts—nine, to be exact. Baseball-building starts from the center, with a small cork ball called the pill. This is surrounded by two thin layers of rubber, one black and one red. Next, three layers of wool yarn are wound around the pill using a sewing machine. The machine adds 150 yards (137 meters) of cotton yarn after that. The ball is then dipped in rubber cement and covered with two strips of white cowhide shaped like figure eights. A person, not a machine, applies the cowhide. A worker stitches the cowhide onto the ball using 108 stitches of red cotton thread.

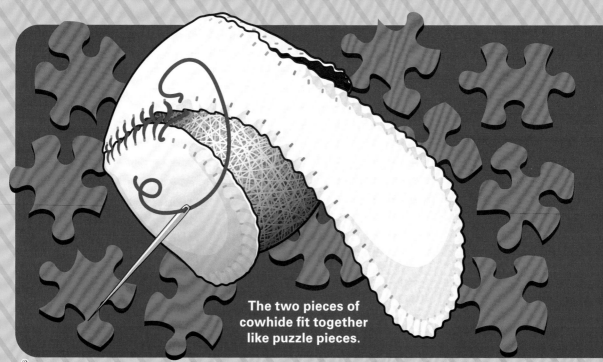

The two pieces of cowhide fit together like puzzle pieces.

Inside a Baseball

red cotton thread

cowhide

black rubber

four-ply gray wool yarn

pill

red rubber

cotton yarn

cowhide

three-ply gray wool yarn

white wool yarn

Baseball Weight

An inspector makes sure the ball weighs between 5 to 5.25 ounces (142 to 149 grams) and measures 9 to 9.25 inches (23 to 23.5 centimeters) around.

Baseball Circumference

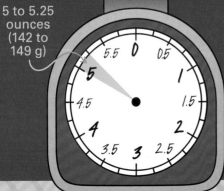

5 to 5.25 ounces (142 to 149 g)

9 to 9.25 inches (23 to 23.5 cm)

THROWN FOR A CURVE

Some people say that hitting a curveball is the hardest thing to do in all of sports. Hitting *any* pitch is hard enough. Even the best big leaguers get a hit only about three out of ten times at bat. When the pitcher has a mean curveball, the odds can get even lower.

Pitchers put spin on a baseball when they throw it. Normally, when you throw a ball, your fingers roll off the top and cause it to spin backward in the air. But to throw a curve, a pitcher spins the ball forward when releasing it. Here's how the spin changes the way a baseball flies toward home plate.

Fastball Path

pitcher's mound

home plate

Curveball Path

pitcher's mound

home plate

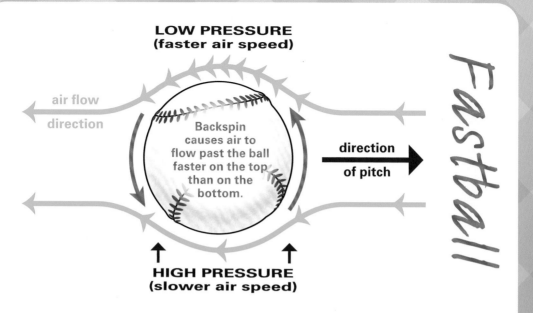

LOW PRESSURE
(faster air speed)

air flow
direction

Backspin
causes air to
flow past the ball
faster on the top
than on the
bottom.

direction
of pitch

HIGH PRESSURE
(slower air speed)

Fastball

When a baseball is thrown with backspin, air flowing more quickly past the top of the ball raises the air pressure under the ball. The air pressure pushes the ball upward, helping it resist gravity and fly straight a bit longer.

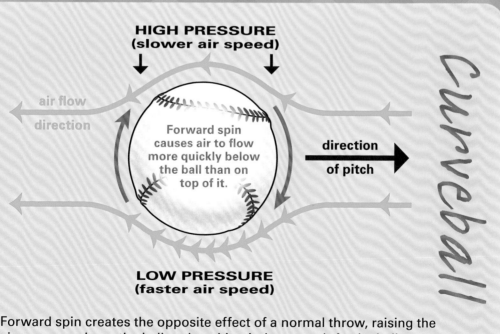

HIGH PRESSURE
(slower air speed)

air flow
direction

Forward spin
causes air to flow
more quickly below
the ball than on
top of it.

direction
of pitch

LOW PRESSURE
(faster air speed)

Curveball

Forward spin creates the opposite effect of a normal throw, raising the air pressure above the ball and pushing it downward. As the ball gets close to the batter, gravity and air pressure work together to make the ball drop suddenly. This makes the ball harder to hit.

BLAZING FASTBALLS

Don't you love the sound of a great fastball? It's almost like the ball sizzles in the air before it pops into the glove.

How fast are those pitches, anyway? Of course, different players have different abilities. And almost everyone can get better with practice. But the graphic below can give you a good idea of what you're facing in the batter's box. It shows the average fastball speed for pitchers from the age of eight up to the pro level. The pitch speeds are taken from a limited sample, so results may vary.

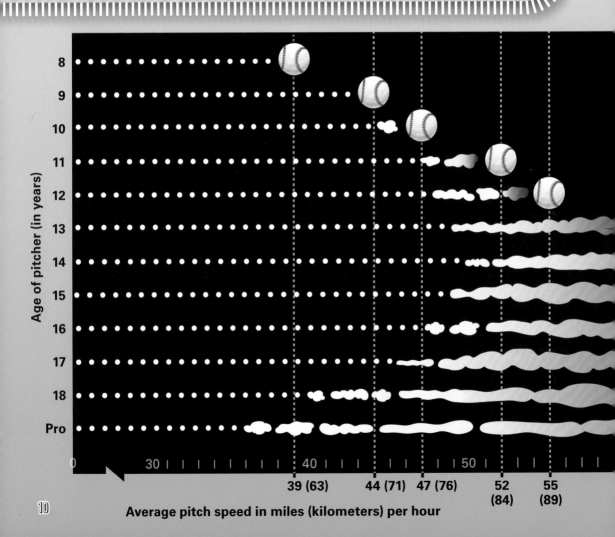

Age of pitcher (in years)

8
9
10
11
12
13
14
15
16
17
18
Pro

0   30   40   50

39 (63)   44 (71)   47 (76)   52   55
                                 (84)   (89)

Average pitch speed in miles (kilometers) per hour

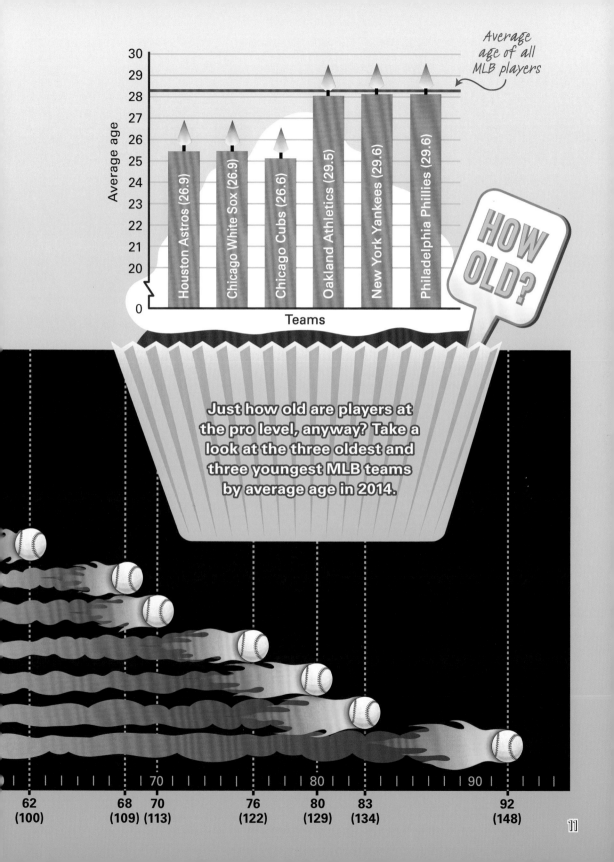

Average age of all MLB players

Average age

30
29
28
27
26
25
24
23
22
21
20
0

Houston Astros (26.9)
Chicago White Sox (26.9)
Chicago Cubs (26.6)
Oakland Athletics (29.5)
New York Yankees (29.6)
Philadelphia Phillies (29.6)

Teams

HOW OLD?

Just how old are players at the pro level, anyway? Take a look at the three oldest and three youngest MLB teams by average age in 2014.

70   80   90

62
(100)

68
(109)

70
(113)

76
(122)

80
(129)

83
(134)

92
(148)

LIFTOFF!

Why is hitting a baseball so hard? After all, almost anyone can swing a bat. But there's a lot going on from the moment the pitcher winds up until the batter finishes swinging. The batter is trying to hit a small baseball with the even smaller sweet spot of the bat. And the batter has to do it in less than half a second. Hitting a home run involves strength, a quick eye, and quicker hands. Here's how everything comes together.

batter

sweet spot

The batter must time the swing to hit the ball with the sweet spot of the bat at exactly the right moment.

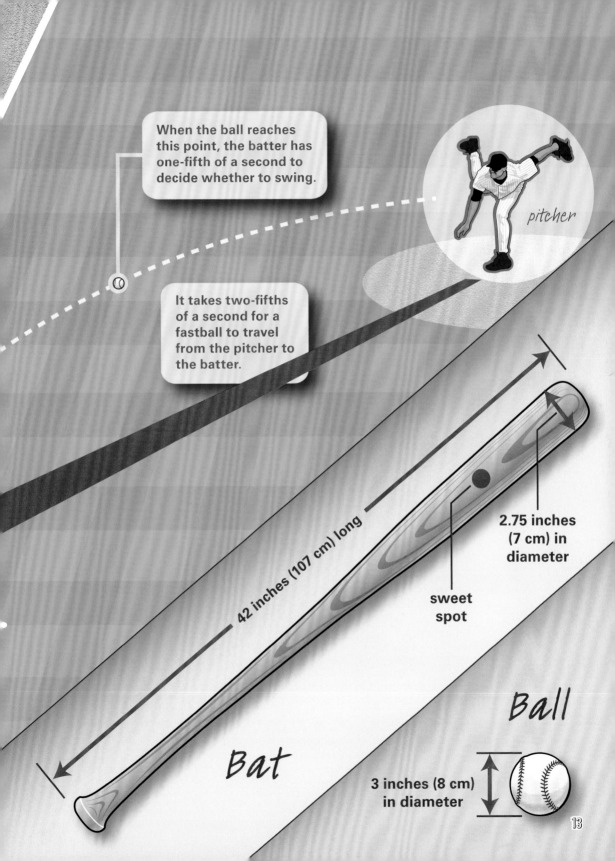

When the ball reaches this point, the batter has one-fifth of a second to decide whether to swing.

pitcher

It takes two-fifths of a second for a fastball to travel from the pitcher to the batter.

2.75 inches (7 cm) in diameter

42 inches (107 cm) long

sweet spot

Bat

Ball

3 inches (8 cm) in diameter

A DAY AT THE PARK

One way baseball is different from other sports is that the field you play on isn't always the same size. In American football, for example, every field has exactly 100 yards (91 m) between the two end zones. But a baseball park can have a wide range of dimensions. And those dimensions can affect the game. So too can a stadium's elevation above sea level and the air temperature in the area. Check out these graphics to see how a park's dimensions and other factors affect games.

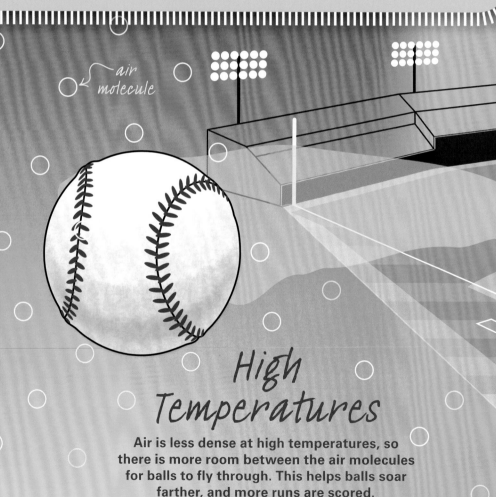

air molecule

High Temperatures

Air is less dense at high temperatures, so there is more room between the air molecules for balls to fly through. This helps balls soar farther, and more runs are scored.

High Elevations

At high elevations, there is less air and therefore fewer air molecules to slow baseballs as they fly.

air molecule

PLAY BALL!

foul pole

outfield fence

Distance

Outfield fences at baseball parks are placed at different distances from home plate. Closer outfield fences mean more home runs and more runs scored.

Height

The height of outfield fences is different from stadium to stadium. Shorter fences mean more home runs and more runs scored.

Foul Territory

Baseball parks have different foul territory dimensions. More foul territory makes it easier for the defense to get outs because there's more room for defenders to catch pop-ups. This means fewer runs scored.

WHAT HAPPENS TO BALLS IN PLAY?

In the major leagues, a batter's chance of getting a hit depends a lot on how the ball flies off his bat. Did he smash a line drive or knock a lazy fly ball into the sky? Did he hit a ground ball that the infielders can easily scoop up? This chart shows how often balls put into play in MLB result in fly balls, line drives, and ground balls. You can also see the rate at which each type of batted ball results in a base hit or an out.

79%
of fly balls
become
OUTS

21%
of fly balls
become
HITS

26%
of line drives
become
OUTS

74%
of line drives
become
HITS

36%
of balls put
in play are
**FLY
BALLS**

20%
of balls put
in play are
**LINE
DRIVES**

44%
of balls put
in play are
**GROUND
BALLS**

72%
of ground balls
become
OUTS

28%
of ground
balls become
HITS

THE MOST EXCITING PLAY IN BASEBALL

Some might argue that the home run is the most exciting play in baseball. But regular home runs are fairly common. If the batter pops it out of the park, he just trots around the bases. Where's the drama in that? An inside-the-park homer is a different story, though. The batter scalds a line drive deep into the outfield. He runs hard to first base, thinking he'll stretch the hit into a double. He watches the outfielders go after the ball and realizes he has time to make it to third base. Then he rounds third! He's heading home! Here comes the throw—will he make it? Some big leaguers have put on this exciting show for the fans quite a few times. Here are MLB's career leaders in inside-the-park homers (and the years each player played).

Rogers Hornsby (1915–1937)

Edd Roush (1913–1931)

Jake Daubert (1910–1924)

Willie Keeler (1892–1910)

Number of inside-the-park home runs

Jesse "the Crab" Burkett (1890–1905)

Sam Crawford (1899–1917)

Tommy Leach
(1898–1918)

Ty Cobb
(1905–1928)

Honus Wagner
(1897–1917)

Jake Beckley (1888–1907)

Tris Speaker (1907–1928)

40   45   50   55

HEIGHT ADVANTAGE?

On August 19, 1951, Eddie Gaedel headed to bat for the St. Louis Browns wearing uniform number 1/8. The pitcher, Bob Cain, walked him on four pitches—all high. Why was Gaedel so hard to pitch to?

He was 3 feet 7 inches tall (1.1 m), about the height of an average five-year-old boy. A person that short has a very small strike zone. No wonder Cain walked him. Gaedel was the shortest player in MLB history, though he had only one plate appearance. Once he walked, he was pulled from the game and replaced with a pinch runner. He never set foot on a major-league field again.

The average
MLB player
in the 1870s:
5 feet 7 inches
(1.7 m)

The shortest
player in
MLB history:
Eddie Gaedel
(St. Louis
Browns)
3 feet 7 inches
(1.1 m)

The shortest MLB
player in 2014:
Jose Altuve
(Houston Astros)
5 feet 5 inches
(1.7 m)

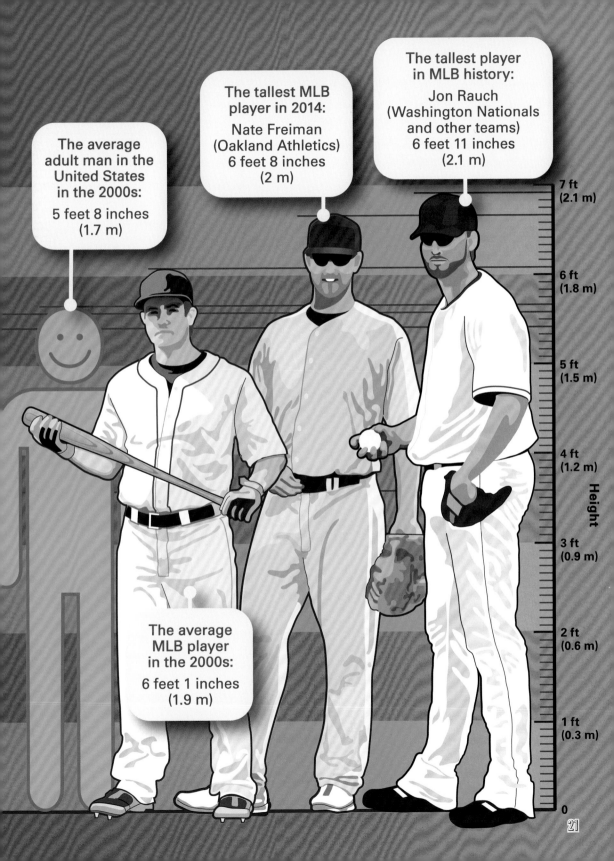

The average adult man in the United States in the 2000s: 5 feet 8 inches (1.7 m)

The tallest MLB player in 2014: Nate Freiman (Oakland Athletics) 6 feet 8 inches (2 m)

The tallest player in MLB history: Jon Rauch (Washington Nationals and other teams) 6 feet 11 inches (2.1 m)

The average MLB player in the 2000s: 6 feet 1 inches (1.9 m)

7 ft (2.1 m)
6 ft (1.8 m)
5 ft (1.5 m)
4 ft (1.2 m)
3 ft (0.9 m)
2 ft (0.6 m)
1 ft (0.3 m)
0

Height

IT PAYS TO PLAY

It must be nice to be a big leaguer. Not only do you get to play baseball all the time, but you get paid—a lot. With all the money coming in from TV, ticket sales, and merchandise sales, teams can easily afford big player salaries. And those salaries have been rising fast the past couple of decades, as you can see in this timeline. It highlights MLB's highest-paid players every 10 years since 1874.

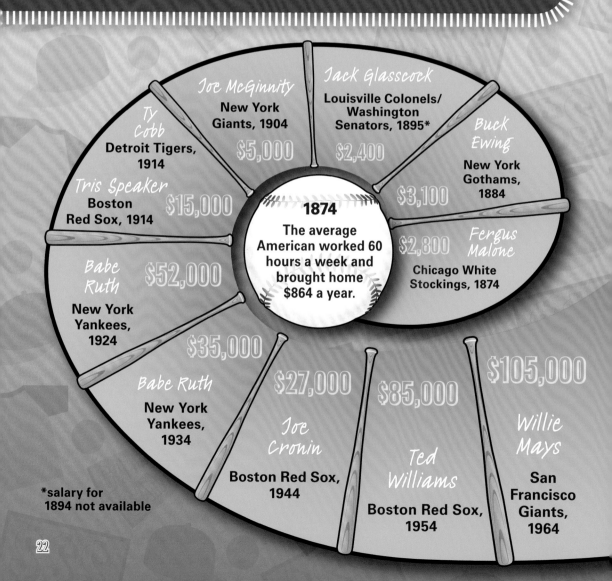

Joe McGinnity
New York Giants, 1904
$5,000

Jack Glasscock
Louisville Colonels/ Washington Senators, 1895*
$2,400

Ty Cobb
Detroit Tigers, 1914

Buck Ewing
New York Gothams, 1884
$3,100

Tris Speaker
Boston Red Sox, 1914
$15,000

1874
The average American worked 60 hours a week and brought home $864 a year.

$2,800
Fergus Malone
Chicago White Stockings, 1874

Babe Ruth
New York Yankees, 1924
$52,000

$35,000

Babe Ruth
New York Yankees, 1934

$27,000
Joe Cronin
Boston Red Sox, 1944

$85,000
Ted Williams
Boston Red Sox, 1954

$105,000
Willie Mays
San Francisco Giants, 1964

*salary for 1894 not available

Zack
Greinke
Los Angeles Dodgers, 2014

$26,000,000

2012
The average
American earned
about $42,000
a year.

$21,726,881

Alex
Rodriguez
**New York Yankees,
2004**

$6,300,000

Bobby
Bonilla
**New York Mets,
1994**

$1,989,875

Mike
Schmidt
**Philadelphia
Phillies,
1984**

$250,000

Dick Allen
**Chicago White Sox,
1974**

HELLO, WORLD

Every MLB team has the same goal during the season: to win the World Series. But while every team is after the same prize, only one team per year actually achieves it. The first professional baseball championship was played in 1884. That year, the National League's (NL) Providence Grays defeated the New York Metropolitan Baseball Club of the American Association. By 1901, the American Association had become the American League (AL).

In 1903, the top AL team—the Boston Americans—faced off against the top NL team—the Pittsburgh Pirates. Boston won this first World Series. Since then, the World Series has been played almost every year, producing 108 champs.

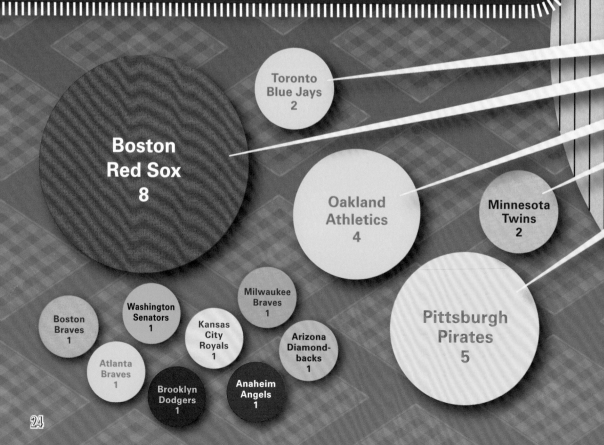

Toronto Blue Jays 2

Boston Red Sox 8

Oakland Athletics 4

Minnesota Twins 2

Boston Braves 1

Washington Senators 1

Kansas City Royals 1

Milwaukee Braves 1

Arizona Diamond-backs 1

Pittsburgh Pirates 5

Atlanta Braves 1

Brooklyn Dodgers 1

Anaheim Angels 1

GLOBAL BASEBALL

Baseball was invented in the United States and is still considered America's national pastime, but the sport has gained popularity all around the world. Many of the biggest MLB stars are from other countries. In fact, in 2014, more than one-fourth of all MLB players were from a country other than the United States. The numbers on the map represent how many players were on MLB rosters from the countries shown as of April 1, 2014, including the United States.

South Korea
2

Japan
9

Taiwan
2

Australia
2

FANS DIG THE LONG BALL

Nothing makes a pitcher more nervous than when a power hitter steps up to the plate. Power hitters can put runs on the board with one swing of the bat. The pitcher takes a deep breath and blows it out. He winds up. He reaches back. He fires the ball toward the plate, and . . . *BOOM!* It's a home run! A dinger! A tater! There are lots of fun nicknames for baseball's most impressive display of power. Take a look at the men who have hit the most MLB home runs of all time.

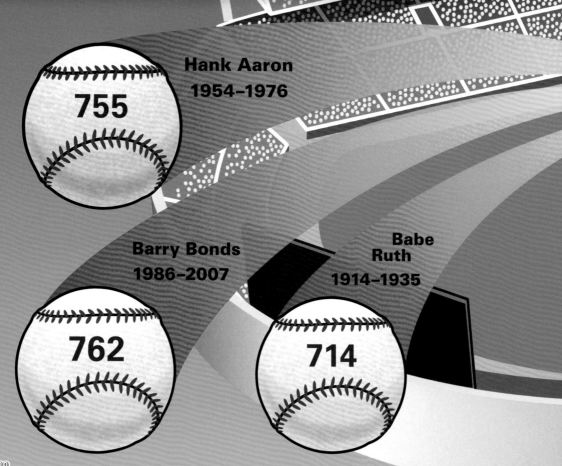

Hank Aaron
1954–1976
755

Barry Bonds
1986–2007
762

Babe Ruth
1914–1935
714

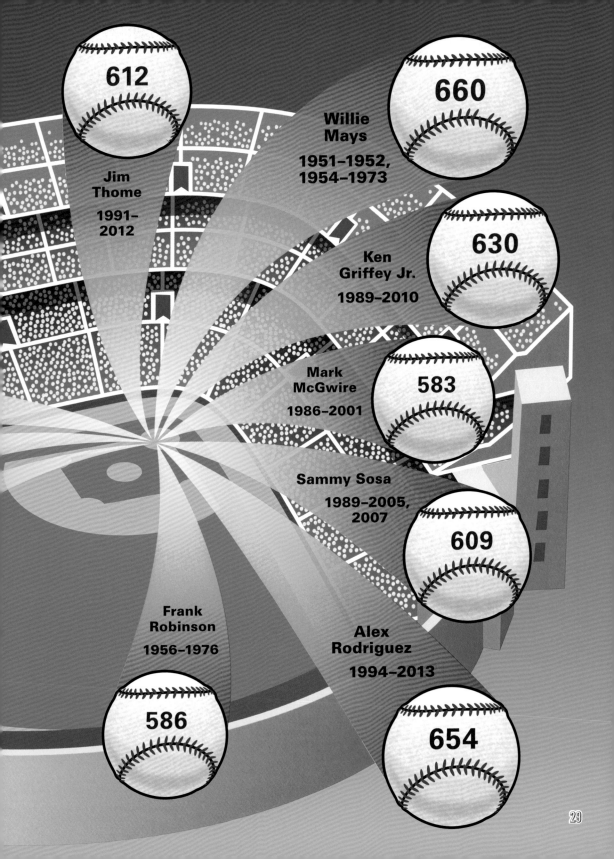

612

Jim
Thome

1991–
2012

Willie
Mays

1951–1952,
1954–1973

660

Ken
Griffey Jr.

1989–2010

630

Mark
McGwire

1986–2001

583

Sammy Sosa

1989–2005,
2007

609

Frank
Robinson

1956–1976

Alex
Rodriguez

1994–2013

586

654

Glossary

AMERICAN ASSOCIATION: a professional baseball league that began in 1882

BACKSPIN: when a baseball in motion spins so the bottom rotates forward and the top rotates backward

CURVEBALL: a pitch that spins down and away from a batter as it approaches

DIAMETER: the width of a circular object

DIMENSIONS: the measurements of something's size

ELEVATION: the height of a place above sea level

FASTBALL: a rapid, relatively straight pitch

FOUL TERRITORY: the area on a baseball field outside the first- and third-base lines. If a ball is hit in foul territory, it is not a fair hit.

LINE DRIVE: a ball that is batted in a straight line

MERCHANDISE: goods that are bought or sold. MLB merchandise usually has an MLB team logo.

MOLECULE: the smallest unit of something

PINCH RUNNER: a replacement base runner

SALARY: the amount of money someone is paid for work, not including bonuses

SWEET SPOT: a spot in the barrel of a baseball bat. Hitting a ball on the sweet spot results in less vibration to the hitter's hands and more power transferring to the ball

Further Information

Baseball Reference
http://www.baseball-reference.com
This is the best source for baseball statistics you can find—with stats for every player in the history of the game. It's a critical reference for anyone who studies the game seriously.

Donovan, Sandy. *Sports Top Tens.* Minneapolis: Lerner Publications, 2015. Read about history-makers and record-breakers from a variety of sports in this fun book.

Exploratorium—Science of Baseball
http://www.exploratorium.edu /baseball/index.html
This Exploratorium website goes deep into the science of baseball.

Jacobs, Greg. *The Everything Kids' Baseball Book: From Baseball's History to Today's Favorite Players— Lots of Home Run Fun in Between!* New York: Adams Media, 2014. Learn all kinds of interesting baseball facts in this fun book.

Kelley, James E. *Baseball.* Eyewitness Book series. New York: DK, 2010. This book provides a broad look at America's national pastime.

Kennedy, Mike, and Mark Stewart. *Long Ball: The Legend and Lore of the Home Run.* Minneapolis: Millbrook Press, 2006. Find out more about America's pastime through stories, stats, and amazing photos.

Major League Baseball
http://mlb.mlb.com/home
MLB is the main source for news about big-league baseball and the best baseball players in the world.

Nelson, Kadir. *We Are the Ship: The Story of Negro League Baseball.* New York: Jump at the Sun, 2008. This beautiful picture book tells the story of the Negro Leagues, an important part of baseball's history.

Sports Illustrated. *Sports Illustrated Baseball's Greatest.* New York: Sports Illustrated, 2013. SI's editors compiled fascinating top 10 lists: top 10 all-time best shortstops, top 10 best catchers, top 10 best relief pitchers, top 10 best sluggers, and more.

Index